Living Intentionally before God

Living Intentionally before God

Reflections on 1 Thessalonians

Paul S. Jeon

WIPF & STOCK · Eugene, Oregon

LIVING INTENTIONALLY BEFORE GOD
Reflections on 1 Thessalonians

Wipf & Stock
An Imprint of Wipf and Stock Publishers
199 W. 8th Ave., Suite 3
Eugene, OR 97401
www.wipfandstock.com

ISBN 13: 978-1-62032-661-9
Manufactured in the U.S.A.

All Scripture quotations are the author's own translation.

This work is dedicated to Hyejung Choi,
our heroine.

Contents

Foreword

Mankind has always been fascinated by notions of superheroes and fantasies. The oldest stories known to mankind have always featured gods, demi-gods, or heroes, usually in a world where good and evil is clearly defined. In today's world, the most popular movies are superhero movies and the most popular books are fantasy books. Our desire to be great, to be recognized, and to somehow transcend the human frailty seems to be an essential part of who we are. Even as we grow old, we don't quite give up this desire; rather, it manifests itself in different, more subtle forms. We wish to excel in our jobs or other pursuits. We wish to be recognized, if not by the world, at least by our peers and colleagues. We want to play the good guy if we can help it. We want our kids to be gifted and talented.

When Christ calls us to follow him, the first shocking lesson we learn after conversion is that in all of human history, there has only been *one* true Superhero: Jesus Christ, the faithful Son who left his Father and gave up his glory to come down to the earth to save sinners through His death on the Cross. "Every story in the Bible whispers his name," we are told. In fact, we come to recognize that every story mankind has ever known whispers His name in some form or another. Our second shocking lesson—equally difficult to accept—is learning that we are ourselves all superheroes insofar as—and *only* insofar as—the true Superhero lives in us through the Spirit. From God's perspective, the only perspective that matters in the end is that we are His beloved children whose sins have been washed away by the blood Christ shed on the cross. Everything that we ever wished to accomplish ourselves, in its truest form, was already accomplished by Christ and in Christ.

Unfortunately, for most of us, this does not necessarily mean we have successfully renounced ourselves of our own dreams of becoming superheroes. Now that we know the Truth as a person, and as our Savior and Lord, we secretly harbor desires to become super-followers of Christ, or super-Christians. We read about the saints of the old and the miracles they have performed or even persecutions they have withstood, and wonder why such supernatural events are so rare in our life. Much like Jesus's disciples in their early days, we quibble internally about where we might be seated in heaven, and whether we might be closer to Jesus than other Christians we know of.

Now there is nothing wrong with trying to be the best Christians we can possibly be, so long as our hearts are right with God. Our Lord taught us to enter through the narrow gate (Matthew 7:13). Saint Paul taught us to run the race as to win the crown (1 Corinthians 9:24). But there *is* something wrong with trying to fly when we can barely walk, or trying to swallow a steak when we can barely drink milk. We might say that even after learning to follow Christ, we insist upon our own ways of following Him: it is as if we say to Him, "Lord Jesus, I shall follow you, but *on my own term*." For this reason, one of the hardest lessons for Christians is to learn to be faithful over *little*. And yet, Jesus said: "One who is faithful in a very little is also faithful in much, and one who is dishonest in a very little is also dishonest in much" (Luke 16:10). In the next world, perhaps, when we see God face to face, we may very well find ourselves to be flying. Perhaps some of us have already seen glimpses of the next world. For most of us, including myself, progress is far and few between, and certainly less apparent than regresses or lapses.

I read *Living Intentionally* for the first time during a difficult period in my life. Our family had just made a move from one end of the country to the other, and we were beginning a new life in a city we had never been to and with no community in which to grow. My patience level was at an all-time low, when things didn't turn out as expected. I was not a good husband to my wife and even less a good father to my daughter. My walk with Jesus was filled with doubts—not a doubt as to the reality of Jesus Christ but a doubt as to whether I was indeed walking with him, whether I could still hear His call, whether I could return to sensing the joy I used to know in Christ. My prayer life was going through a dry season, and it felt like I wasn't learning anything new—illuminations or teachings—about which to get excited. In fact, in all honesty, if not for Pastor Paul's request, against his better judgment, for me to write this foreword I may not have gotten through it in my state of spiritual stupor. But in reading these devotionals over and over, I came to realize that in seeking God in extraordinary areas, I forgot to seek God in *ordinary* areas. I was asking the wrong questions to guide my life, and perhaps applying an unbiblical method of seeking God. Instead of seeking new illuminations, I should have been faithful to the old teachings; instead of seeking to be a compassionate hero to the world, I should have learned to exercise more love and understanding towards my family; instead of seeking signs from God, I should have been examining within for signs of true conversion. In reading these devotionals I was able to go back to the most basic teachings of the Bible—the lessons Saint Paul taught us by living out—which I had forgotten even to pursue.

You will find no new teachings in *Living Intentionally*, and that is perhaps one of the greatest compliments I can give to a devotional. As a wise man once said, "We do not so much need new teachings in morality as we simply need to be reminded of the old teachings." A baby drinking milk may eventually grow to eat solid food, but no baby can or should ever forget how to drink milk, and milk remains an essential dietary product for all of human life. Likewise, we do not so much need a new theology as we need to be constantly reminded of the Person whom our theology celebrates. We do not so much need new calls from God as we simply need to be reminded of the old calls we have not been obeying.

If you have been going through a dry season with God and are wondering where you stand with Him, this devotional will be particularly helpful to you. Let us not despair for not being able to run a marathon, but let us instead remember the Father who delights in every baby step we take in obedience of His Word. I hope you will find *Living Intentionally* as refreshing as I found it to be. May God bless you in your walk with Christ.

Alex Lee
Assistant Professor of Law,
USC Gould School of LawPasadena, CA

Preface

I NEVER EXPECTED TO write a devotional on 1 Thessalonians, let alone an extensive study (which is due in 2014). So perhaps a word on how the devotional came together may serve the reader.

My father retired early from his dental practice to serve as a missionary in Honduras. I vividly recall asking him why he didn't just retire and spend his days playing golf, traveling, and doing what most people dream of when they think of retirement. His answer was plain and simple: "As Christians we march to a different drummer, which includes the way we think about and approach retirement. We're supposed to be intentional in every season, including the final season God gives us."

During my doctorate studies I came across several extraordinary believers. There are many adjectives I could use to describe them—generous, hilarious, compassionate, and so forth. But perhaps the most fitting adjective is intentional, expressed by a profound and tangible commitment to consider how our call to follow Christ Jesus reshapes every aspect of life. Their lifestyles have exemplified for me and many others what it means to confess Jesus as Lord.

Finally, in the spring of 2012 I had the opportunity to teach an introductory course on Paul's letters at Reformed Theological Seminary. Perhaps because my mind had been attuned to the topic of intentionality I was more sensitive to the theme than in the past. In particular 1 Thessalonians—specifically Paul's commitment to live intentionally for the sake of the gospel—left a deep impression on how all believers are to live. The apostle was so purposeful throughout his ministry among the Thessalonians that he was able to freely declare, "You know how I lived among you" (2:2, 5). After studying the letter in more detail, I resolved to write a brief devotional based on the letter and on the theme of living intentionally. My hope is that the devotional will challenge the reader to consider the importance—the necessity—of this undervalued Christian virtue.

My conviction is that devotionals should be nothing more than thinking God's thoughts after him, that is, their function is simply to amplify the teaching of Scripture itself. I hold revelation in much higher esteem than innovation: what people need to hear is less of me and more of God. Therefore, my hope is the reader will arrive at a deeper understanding of Scripture through the brief comments provided in this devotional.

As always, some thanks are in order. First, I thank my family—dad and mom, Abraham, Mary, David, and Janice. Second, I thank the members of NewCity Church for the privilege to serve as their pastor. I'm especially grateful for Hyejung whose quiet resilience, humility, and strength inspire us all. Finally, I thank my wife and sons for being a source unending joy; I love you all.

Paul S. Jeon
August 26, 2012

1

Reflections on 1:1

Always in the Presence of God the Father and the Lord Jesus Christ

The prescript of the letter, which includes the writers ("Paul, Silas, and Timothy"), the audience ("the church of the Thessalonians"), and greeting ("Grace to you and peace"), sets the stage for the rest of the letter. Paul usually addresses a church by the particular city wherein it dwells—such as "the churches of Galatia" or "the saints in Ephesus." Not so here. In this instance, Paul addresses his immediate audience as "the church of the Thessalonians *in God the Father and the Lord Jesus Christ*." Paul is highlighting the fact that the Thessalonians, as an assembly of people gathered for worship and fellowship, forever live in and before the presence of "God the Father and the Lord Jesus Christ." We may ask why this reminder was necessary on Paul's part.

Paul's intention for the Thessalonians becomes clear when we consider the very circumstances that defined these Thessalonians' lives. As the rest of the letter makes clear, the Thessalonians were undergoing severe persecution—to the point that Paul had become anxious over the possibility of their fall from grace (see 3:1-5). Paul's anxiety, of course, was not unwarranted. After all, is it really far-fetched to suggest that the faith of believers tends to be radically shaken when their circumstances are tumultuous? Whether it's in the form of an uncaring boss, a debilitating condition, or a rocky marriage, our circumstances possess an uncanny ability to raise questions about God's goodness, wisdom, and power. As much as we know that we're called to live by faith—not by sight—the reality is what we see affects what we believe. When all is well, we conclude that God must be good; when all is not well, we begin to wonder whether God is really in control.

We are not too different from the Thessalonians. And so here, from the outset Paul gently reminds the saints that believers are always under the care and protection of "God the Father and the Lord Jesus Christ" through whom they find all-sufficient grace and peace for each day. This promise holds true for all eternity because of Christ Jesus, whose perfect life, atoning death, and vindicating resurrection have won for them God's favor.

Questions for Further Reflection

1. Do you believe that as a Christian you are always in the presence of "God the Father and the Lord Jesus Christ"? How is your confidence in his care and rule expressed during times of struggle? How is your integrity manifested when the only one looking is the Audience of One?

2

Reflections on 1:2

Always in Prayer, Always in Remembrance of the Saints

One truly remarkable trait of Paul was that he always lived the very life he preached. For instance, the declaration "We give thanks to God always" (1:2a) later resurfaces as a command "Give thanks always" (5:18). Similarly, the phrase "constantly making remembrance of you in our prayers" (1:2b) is later echoed in the command "Pray constantly" (5:17). Paul doesn't simply instruct the Thessalonians by his word; rather, he presents himself as a worthy model of the faith to follow.

No doubt Paul's declaration of being in constant prayer for the Thessalonians would have comforted them and established an even stronger bond between Paul and the Thessalonians. Paul was not shy about communicating his deep affection for them, expressed especially in regular prayer on their behalf. But, perhaps more importantly, the words "always" and "constantly" conveyed to the audience that Paul himself was living in regular and intimate communion with God through prayer. As a loving brother in Christ, Paul is here intimating that prayer is the basic means for pursuing a life centered on God the Father and the Lord Jesus Christ.

In addition, Paul introduces here the important theme of remembrance. This theme is repeatedly expressed in various forms—in Paul's remembrance of God's goodness towards the Thessalonians (1:2); in his remembrance of the faith, love, and hope of the Thessalonians (1:3); in his reminder to them of the example he and his colleagues set for them by toiling day and night in order not to be a financial burden to anyone (2:9); in the Thessalonians' remembrance of Paul and his colleagues (3:6); and in the general exhortation to the Thessalonians to remember what they have been taught (4:1-2).

Remembering is an unappreciated but important Christian virtue. A few simple examples from life remind us of the power of this virtue. Marriages are built—not on falling in love—but on remembering the vows that husbands and wives make to each other. Many are motivated to work hard in honor of the sacrifices made by their parents and others on their behalf—in short, in remembrance of others. Christianity generosity is in response to remembering God's overwhelming generosity to us through the sacrifice of His beloved son. In summary, remembering the past has tremendous influence on how we live in the present and future. It's no wonder that Paul begins this letter by highlighting his own remembrance of the Thessalonians in his prayers. In doing so, he will call them to remember and hold tightly to their own confession of faith in the face of persecution.

Questions for Further Reflection

1. Are you in regular and deep communion with God through prayer? How might your life be different if you took regular time (perhaps an hour a week) to engage in the discipline of remembering God and others through prayer?

3

Reflections on 1:3

The Memory of the Thessalonians

VERSE 3 BEGINS WITH Saint Paul remembering several qualities about the Thessalonians that give rise to his thanksgiving in 1:2. Before reflecting on each of these in more detail, we shouldn't miss the overall message that Paul rejoices in the fact that the Thessalonians are authentic believers, as evidenced in the way their faith leads to good works, their love to ceaseless toil, and their hope to perseverance (1:3). Here we do well to consider not only whether we display such signs of life that gladden Paul's heart, but also whether we rejoice when we see them in others. After all, what gets us excited reveals what our hearts holds as precious.

The first two qualities (faith resulting in *works*, love producing *labor*) are related, both centering on some type of industrious effort. The precise "work" and "labor" Paul has in mind is unclear. Is he referring to work and labor done for other believers in Thessalonica or for people in general or even for believers beyond Thessalonica? Nevertheless, one thing is clear: their work and labor were unforgettable. More to the point, such work and labor represented the visible and concrete manifestations of what are otherwise invisible and intangible, namely "faith" and "love." As Paul writes in all his letters, genuine faith in and love for God must be expressed in faithful works and labors of love.

The last quality, which is preserved in the *New American Bible* as "endurance in hope of our Lord Jesus Christ, before our God and Father," requires some explanation. Paul is referring to the quality of perseverance that stems from hope in the Lord Jesus Christ. Such hope is not merely an abstract wish, but a profoundly personal hope in the One who has risen from the dead and is now in the presence of God interceding on our behalf. Hence, a fuller translation would read "endurance from hope in our Lord Jesus Christ who is before our God and Father." Hope for Christians, therefore, is founded on the certainty of someday being in the presence of both the risen Lord Jesus and God the Father. No tribulation in life can rob us from the promise of someday being with the One who laid down His life for us; and it is this truth that empowers believers just the same today as it did the Thessalonians nearly two thousand years ago to endure every trial with joyful expectation.

Questions for Further Reflection

1. Does your life exhibit such signs of life? What are concrete and visible ways your faith, love, and hope are being regularly expressed?

4

Reflections on 1:4–5a

Evident Salvation

SAINT PAUL WAS THANKFUL for the Thessalonians not only because of their work of faith, labor of love, and perseverance of hope (1:3), but also because of their gospel-reception and transformation. Paul writes "the gospel came not only in word but also in power and in the Holy Spirit and in full conviction" (1:5a). There's no need here to parse the meaning of each phrase in the statement. Paul's point is that their acceptance of gospel resulted in a noticeable change described in terms of "power" and "the Holy Spirit" and "full conviction." That is, their embrace of the gospel expressed itself in the conviction that life must change *radically* if the gospel is true. This transformation, in turn, assured Paul of their elect status as those loved by God (1:4).

Verse 4 suggests that Paul regularly sought to identify Spiritual fruit that evidenced genuine gospel-conversion. For Paul Jesus's exhortation to "first take the log out of your own eye" (Matthew 7:5a) did not mean that believers should not seek to discern fruit in the lives of other saints. Genuine conversion is too important of a matter to be wrong about. Therefore, like Paul, we ought to regularly and humbly consider whether the saints are showing signs of new life in Christ Jesus.

To be sure, gospel-conviction comes out in different ways. For one person it may mean packing his bags and leaving his comforts to move to a country where his skills can be used to help the poor.

For another it may mean living humbly—despite a high salary—so that he has more to give. For yet another, it may simply mean resolving to stop gossiping. Whatever the form, conviction expressed in changed living gives evidence of true salvation.

Questions for Further Reflection

1. Do you regularly look for "signs of life"—that is, evidence of your salvation? Do you regularly look for "signs of life" in other professing Christians? Why or why not? Why is it important that we engage in such introspection for ourselves and others?

5

Reflections on 1:5b–8

The Spread of the Gospel through Intentional Living

NOWADAYS THERE'S NO SHORTAGE of literature on church growth. Some of it is helpful, some less. But whenever we rely unduly on "church specialists," there's the danger of forgetting the obvious. The spread of the gospel didn't depend on fancy facilities, loud music, and charismatic speakers. Rather, the gospel spread, and continues to spread, by way of personal example.

The Thessalonians received the gospel with much conviction, but their conviction was a result of the supernatural working through the natural. Paul reminds the Thessalonians of how he and his colleagues lived among them for their sake. Knowing that their manner of life could be either a help or hindrance to the cause of the gospel, they made a concerted effort to pursue irreproachable lives. Paul was so intentional about this that he was able to write with confidence, "You know what sort of men we were among you for your sake" (1:5).

As a result not only did the Thessalonians become "imitators of [Paul] and of the Lord" by receiving the word in much affliction but with the joy of the Holy Spirit (1:6), but they in turn became models to all the believers in Macedonia and Achaia (1:7), and their faith went forth everywhere (1:8). Paul knows that the miracle of conversion is ultimately the work of God (1:4). Yet, he's also cognizant of the tremendous impact one's lifestyle can have on the spread of the gospel. Do we desire to see the gospel go forth everywhere?

Then we must be equally serious about living intentionally for the sake of others so that they too will receive the gospel with much conviction. As one apologist wrote, "Let your life be your best argument for the Christian faith."

Questions for Further Reflection

1. How does your life serve as a help or hindrance to others' receiving the gospel? Do you find yourself living intentionally for the sake of others? Is your life a compelling witness to the gospel?

6

Reflections on 1:9–10

Marks of True Conversion

WHAT ARE THE MARKS of true conversion? This is a much debated point. Some say it's praying in tongues; others say it's a joyful heart; still others say it's how much time you devote to reading the Bible. Today's passage teaches us there are at least two aspects of true conversion—a new direction and a new disposition.

The great songwriter Bob Dylan once wrote a song titled "Gotta Serve Somebody." Its chorus goes: "Well, it may be the devil or it may be the Lord / But you're gonna have to serve somebody." In today's world, there's a widespread belief that somehow we can be "free" people. The truth is that everyone is serving someone or something.

Paul assumes this when writing that the Thessalonians turned *from* serving idols *to* serving the true and living God (1:9). Conversion, then, entails a new direction in life. For many, their previous idols might have been love, money, success, power, recognition, and so forth. These are all fine in and of themselves—until they become ultimate things. The first mark of true conversion is that our focus, energy, time, and daydreaming take on a new direction, turning from these previous idols to the one true God. For the Thessalonians, this internal change in direction became so apparent that others could not help but proclaim how different they had become (1:9a). All true converts in Christ should in due time exhibit such profound changes.

The second mark of true conversion is a new disposition. The word "disposition" is best described as a prevailing mood or outlook. For instance, the disposition of many people in their twenties may be towards marriage; the disposition of many people in their thirties and forties may be towards retirement. But for those who have turned to serve the living and true God, their new disposition is towards the return of God's Son, Jesus, who was raised from the dead and who will deliver us from the coming wrath (1:10). A true convert is one who earnestly anticipates this return and, in the meanwhile, pursues a life that conforms to such anticipation.

Question for Further Reflection

1. Are the marks of a new direction and new disposition evident in your life? Would others be able to "proclaim" how you've radically changed in terms of where you exert your time, energy, money, efforts, and daydreams?

7

Reflections on 2:1–2

Conviction Convicts

Do people have a more difficult time with the message of the gospel or its messengers? How many times have we heard people say, "If they really believe Jesus is the Son of God who died and was raised to life, why then do they live the way they do? Shouldn't their lives be different—more purposeful?" Indeed, should we not expect our belief in Jesus to result in a noticeably distinct lifestyle?

Saint Paul comments that his visit to the Thessalonians was not in vain (2:1), as evidenced by their undeniable conversion (1:9-10). While acknowledging the decisive role of God's election in their conversion (1:4), Paul is careful to observe the contributing influence of his conviction and perseverance on their acceptance of the gospel. Specifically, Paul highlights how he, Silas, and Timothy proclaimed the gospel of God in the face of much opposition even after having suffered in Philippi (2:2). Recall how they were, at various points in their ministry, dragged into the marketplace, attacked by crowds, stripped, beaten with rods, and imprisoned with their feet in stocks (Acts 16:19-40). This would have been enough to cause many to cower away from sharing the gospel of God; yet Paul remained faithful, knowing that his sufferings and wounds for the gospel would reflect his sincerity and lend more creditability to his message.

Paul is careful to note, however, that their boldness came from the Lord ("we spoke courageously in our God"). By doing so, he reminds the Thessalonians of how the success of his missionary work was ultimately the result of God's empowerment. Left to themselves, Paul and his colleagues—like any normal person—would have cowered away from gospel-ministry. It was God who enabled them through the Spirit of Christ to carry out what therefore became a truly supernatural ministry. It is perhaps for this reason that we sometimes experience the most fruitfulness in our personal ministries in times of weakness, for it is during these seasons we begin to rely on the Lord to accomplish the work He has called us to.

Questions for Further Reflection

1. Are you intentional about suffering well? Do you consider how your conduct in seasons of sorrow and disappointment makes the gospel more or less credible? Do you have the tendency to give up quickly? How might Paul's reliance on God's power inspire you to persevere in your personal ministry?

8

Reflections on 2:3–4

God-Pleasers versus People-Pleasers

THE FIRST IMAGE SAINT Paul uses to describe his ministry is a God-pleaser. A God-pleaser is an individual, much like Paul, whose preoccupation is to please God rather than people (2:4b). To appreciate Paul's description of his ministry we need to first understand the cultural background of the Thessalonians. In this period there was no shortage of itinerant philosophers, rhetoricians, and charlatans who went about the Greek world selling their services and ideas to their followers. In short, they were leeches who took advantage of their devotees. In sharp contrast, Paul's ministry to the Thessalonians did not stem from manipulation, greed, and deceit (2:3). There was nothing Paul was seeking to gain from his audience; rather, his sole desire was to give to them abundantly even in the face of opposition. Such purity in personal ministry is all the more important today given we live in an era when many suspect there must be ulterior motives for every kind deed.

Such purity and integrity are possible when a conscious decision is made to live before God who has called us into the service of Christ. God considered Paul and his colleagues to be trustworthy of gospel-ministry (2:4a); in response to this entrustment, Paul and his colleagues made it their ambition to please the One who had commissioned them and who knows their hearts (2:4b). Their lives were very intentional—not directed towards fearing, manipulating, or pleasing (2:2-4a) people, but on pleasing the One who has called them into their Kingdom through the Son.

It is indeed impossible to serve others with pure and good motivations until we have made a commitment to serve and please God. When we serve others out of fear and greed, the real person serviced is the self, as our goal is to gain something from those we seemingly serve. But when our focus is on pleasing the One who has already made us righteous and pure through Christ Jesus, we are free and empowered to serve according to righteousness and purity. May we strive to become God-pleasers versus people-pleasers in every facet of life!

Questions for Further Reflection

1. What are your motivations in personal ministry? Are you a people-pleaser or a God-pleaser? Can you echo with Paul that your encouragement does not come from manipulation, impurity, and deceit? Or are there selfish motives you need to repent of? Do you believe that in order to love others well, we must first love God?

9

Reflections on 2:5–9

Nursing and Laboring Mother versus Burden

THE SECOND IMAGE SAINT Paul uses to describe his ministry is a nursing mother. The first two verses (2:5-6) echo his earlier comments in 2:3. He notes again how he, together with Silas and Timothy, never spoke with words of flattery or with a pretext for greed. In addition, he highlights how they were so purposeful about pursuing integrity that both God ("God is witness") and the Thessalonians themselves ("you all know") could attest to their integrity. Paul's emphasis on character is a much-needed reminder that personal ministry entails more than the performance of certain duties. Rather, it is a call to continually examine and refine our motivations and goals in light of our relationship with Christ Jesus.

Paul presents a powerful contrast to the greedy and self-seeking person by using the image of a nursing mother caring tenderly for her own. Paul's ministry to the Thessalonians was especially astounding in that he could have been a legitimate burden to them given his apostolic status (2:6). Nevertheless, in the way mothers seek to give themselves entirely to their infants Paul sought to treat the Thessalonians as his own children and, therefore, chose to "labor and toil night and day" so not to be a financial burden to them (2:7, 9). Indeed, his love for them was so great that his desire was to share not only the gospel of God but also of his entire self (2:8). In contemporary terms, he did much more than preach a sermon and return home to his comfortable abode. Rather, he *immersed* himself into the lives of the Thessalonians.

This passage is worthwhile to reflect over for men whose approach to ministry is not dissimilar to that of a stereotypical football coach. To be sure, there is a place in ministry for the kind of tough love a coach exhibits. Still, Paul's example challenges us to consider the selflessness and sacrifice of nursing mothers as an additional inspiration for our ministries. Their example, after all, simply points to the selflessness and sacrifice of Christ Jesus—in a sense, the ultimate nursing mother—who freely surrendered His glory and toiled to the point of death so that we could be made children of God.

A special thanks to the many mothers whose personal examples have made such an analogy possible.

Questions for Further Reflection

1. Are you purposeful in personal ministry? In what ways are you regularly checking your motivations and goals? Are others able to attest to your integrity in ministry? More importantly, could you call God as your witness to your personal purity? Think of the many ways mothers give of themselves for the sake of their children. More importantly, think of Christ Jesus as the ultimate nursing mother. How does the image challenge you to redefine some aspects of your personal ministry? In what ways can you seek to be more "motherly" irrespective of your gender?

10

Reflections on 2:10–12

Inspiring and Instructive Father versus Sycophant

THE THIRD IMAGE SAINT Paul uses in this section to describe his ministry is an exemplary and encouraging father. The first verse (2:10) reiterates his earlier comments in 2:3 and 2:5. He notes again how both the Thessalonians and God are witnesses to how differently, how righteously, and how blamelessly Paul and his colleagues conducted themselves among the saints for their sake, thus amplifying the characteristics of Jesus's own ministry. In reading this passage, we cannot help but feel the *intensity* of their intentionality: they sought to be above reproach in every sense in order to progress faith in God. Intentionality—living purposefully—is a trademark of mature Christians.

Paul's earlier reference to flatters, moneygrubbers, and egotists (2:5) provides the context for appreciating the description of his ministry in 2:11-12. Paul compares his ministry to a healthy relationship between a father and his children. Such a relationship involves instruction, encouragement, and warning. In this sense, Paul's ministry was not self-seeking. His goal was not to elicit approval, money, and glory from the Thessalonians, but to love them by speaking words of truth. Indeed, biblical love speaks truth even when such instruction, encouragement, and warning may create awkwardness and tension.

The basis of Paul's words of faith was God, who had called the Thessalonians into his kingdom and glory through faith in Jesus

Christ. Many of us have experienced the privilege of being invited to join a team or organization. With such an invitation comes all the current and benefits of being a member. The charge given, in turn, is to be a good representative: "Don't do anything that would embarrass us!" Similarly, Paul's exhortation to believers is to examine their lifestyles carefully, considering whether they are living in a manner that is worthy of the One who has called them to serve his kingdom and glory. As citizens of heaven in Christ, we are to be purposeful in everything we say and do in order to honor our Lord and Savior.

A special thanks to the many fathers whose personal examples have made such an analogy possible.

Questions for Further Reflection

1. Think of the many ways fathers ought to inspire and instruct their children. How does the image challenge you to redefine some aspects of your personal ministry in view of God's call into His glory and kingdom? In what ways can you seek to be more "fatherly" as exemplified by Paul?

11

Reflections on 2:13

Right Posture towards the Word

READING THE BIBLE IS a widespread requirement for many freshmen in college. The Bible is considered one of many literary works from the ancient world. For many, it is inspiring, interesting, and even offensive—but nothing more or less than that. In short, many view the Bible as a work of mankind for mankind, and there is nothing divine or supernatural about it.

In reflecting over his ministry to the Thessalonians, Saint Paul understood that his gospel proclamation could have easily been received simply as the words of one man to another. After all, during this period there was no shortage of itinerant speakers who often came with new ideas and persuasive speech. Nevertheless, Paul's unique claim was his apostleship—that he was one commissioned from God to speak on God's behalf. Therefore, although there was nothing supernatural about the medium through which God spoke, the very words—in a mysterious way—were nevertheless anything but natural. For this reason Paul gives thanks for the Thessalonians who received his proclamation not as the words of men but as it really is—the word of God (2:13). Indeed, the manner in which they received the word reflected the genuineness of their faith.

Even many professing Christians today approach the Bible merely for inspiration. Certainly, the Bible has an extraordinary way of moving the soul with lofty thoughts no eye has seen and no mind can conceive. But healthy inspiration can come only when we first receive the Word as it really is—the word of God. As such, it is first and foremost God's authoritative revelation of himself to us and a clear expression of how we are to live in light of his holiness and love. The appropriate posture we are to have, then, is that of an eager student, seeking to know more about God and how we should conform our lives to his will. To be sure, many in this world will fail to comprehend such a disposition, perhaps even taunting us as naïve and gullible. But for us who believe, the Bible is our surest guide for living purposefully in light of the person and work of Jesus Christ.

Question for Further Reflection

1. Take some time to think about and articulate your view on the nature and function of the Bible. Do you view it as God's revelation concerning himself and how we are to honor him? Or do you think it's simply one of many wonderful ancient works? How will these different views affect the way you approach life?

12

Reflections on 2:14–16

Suffering for the Gospel

When we suffer for the sake of the gospel, our resolve to live entirely for Jesus sometimes weakens, and suddenly life feels more confusing. Today's passage offers several insights into gospel-suffering that will hopefully help anchor our faith in the face of turbulence.

First, we should not be surprised if our compatriots today despise, ridicule, and perhaps even persecute us for our faith. This is what happened to the Jews in Judea and to the believers in Thessalonica (2:14-15). Turning from former gods to serve the living and true God involves a significant shift in allegiance. Former compatriots will ridicule our belief in the Bible as the revealed and authoritative word of God; they will laugh at our hope of sharing in the resurrection life of Jesus; and they may even become hostile towards us for failing to share their ideologies and goals. In fact, Jesus himself spoke clearly that suffering for the sake of the gospel is inevitable for true believers (Matthew 5:11).

Second, persevering in suffering—holding to the truth of the gospel and living accordingly—is evidence that God's word is working in us who believe (2:13b). Have you ever wondered, "How do I know for sure that I am saved, that I am a true believer?" Some will appeal to their emotional experience at a retreat or revival. Others will talk about how they come from a Christian home. The Bible provides more secure ways to assess the sincerity of our faith, one of which is whether we persevere in the manner of our spiritual predecessors who were faithful even to the point of death.

Finally, in our suffering we should find comfort in God's justice. Verses 15-16 have sometimes been misunderstood and misapplied as the basis for anti-Semitism. Paul here is following a prophetic tradition that criticized certain Jewish leaders who had persecuted God's prophets. Also, the mention of "God's wrath" (2:16) is likely a reference to a historical event where Jewish leaders were deported to Rome versus some general divine condemnation against all Jews. Paul's point here—keeping in mind the overall context and his main concern to encourage and inspire the Thessalonians—is that God is not blind to those who oppose His gospel and will bring about justice, whether partially in this life or fully on the Day of Judgment. And because *He* is the One who will punish according to His perfect justice, there is no need for followers of Jesus in any generation to take the sword of justice into their own hands. Rather, as Christ trusted in God for vindication, so too His followers are to trust in God for justice and abstain from any form of violence.

Questions for Further Reflection

1. Are you surprised when you suffer for the gospel? If so, take time to explore some assumptions you might have regarding what it means to follow Christ. How does the promise of God's justice bring both comfort and confidence? How does it help remove the desire to take justice into your own hands?

13

Reflections on 2:17–20

Investing Well

THE CHRISTIAN LIFE IS often portrayed in terms of sacrifice—and rightly so. But such sacrifice is not the same as altruism—as if believers have nothing to gain. Jesus himself compared the Christian life to a man who discovered great treasure and sold all he had to buy it (Matthew 13:44). Indeed, much is lost for the sake of Christ and the gospel; but much more is gained, to the extent that all suffering and pain in this life cannot compare with the glory that will be ours when Jesus returns. In today's passage, we are reminded to invest in light of future glory.

Saint Paul begins this passage by recalling the imagery of parenting used earlier in chapter two. A literal translation of 2:17 reads, "But we, brothers, were orphaned of you for a brief time." The verb "to make an orphan" reiterated for the Thessalonians how precious they were to Paul and his colleagues—comparable, in fact, to children. Paul goes on to describe them as his "hope," "joy," "crown" and "glory" before the Lord Jesus Christ (2:19-20). To Paul, the Thessalonians embody his crown of achievement that he will someday set before Jesus. That is, the Thessalonians represent the "return" on his investment: they are an expression of where and how Paul invested all his time, money, and energy for the sake of the gospel.

We can demonstrate our allegiance to Christ through the distinct way we spend our time and money. Many people daydream about the car they've always wanted, the house they've been saving for, and the clothes they'll wear once they make it big. As followers of Jesus, we believe that only what is done for Christ will last and that we should therefore seek to invest in people with the intent of winning them for the gospel. In short, like Paul, we are called to pursue crowns of everlasting glory.

In pursuing our crowns, however, we must not forget the presence of a foe who is perpetually committed to sinking our investments. Just as Satan thwarted Paul and his colleagues' efforts to visit the Thessalonians despite their deep desire to go (2:18), Satan is always at work to keep us from pursuing, developing, and maintaining gospel-driven relationships. Therefore, our investments in souls require tremendous intentionality and persistence. We should not be surprised by obstacles and we should not be too discouraged by setbacks. Christ will not forget our efforts to honor him through the relationships we foster for the sake of the gospel.

Questions for Further Reflection

1. How are you investing for eternity? How are you intentional especially in your relationships? Do you pursue new relationships for the sake of Christ? Do you tend to give up quickly on these relationships or to remain steadfast? How does adopting a spiritual perspective on relationships (e.g., the work of Satan, the faithfulness of Christ) impact the way you persevere in relationships?

14

Reflections on 3:1–5

Spiritual Investments

Those who invest in stock markets tend to review their investment portfolios obsessively as the markets fluctuate. At the very least they want to make sure they haven't lost their principal investments. Saint Paul exhibits a similar type of concern for his spiritual investment in the Thessalonians. Twice in the passage he notes that his anxiety over their faith brought him to a state of "being unable to bear it any longer" (3:1, 5a). Thus, he sent Timothy to determine whether they were persevering in the face of persecution and to further establish and exhort them in their faith (3:2-3). Paul was afraid that Satan had tempted them beyond their ability to endure, bringing to naught all the labor he and his colleagues had invested in the Thessalonians (3:5b).

Here we see Paul's noticeable and genuine concern for his spiritual investments. How different our lives and churches might look today if we adopted a similar concern for the people we have invested in for the gospel! Perhaps our lives would be filled with fewer hobbies as we focus more of our time and energy on initiating new relationships and maintaining old ones. Perhaps churches would be less concerned about numbers *per se* and more focused on discipleship relationships. Today's passage calls us to develop and regularly review our "spiritual investments."

There are several simple applications to consider. First, technological advancements have made staying in touch easier than ever. A simple email to know the spiritual health of partners in the gospel can go a long way. A handwritten letter, of course, is even better. Second, we should have a special concern for believers who are suffering for the gospel. Notice how Paul provides a brief encouragement in verses 3-4, reminding the Thessalonians that all believers are destined to suffer because of their faith. Third, care for our "spiritual investments" requires sacrifice. Paul chose to be bereft of Timothy so that the Thessalonians, in turn, could be encouraged by his presence and ministry. Similarly, encouraging those in need almost always involves sacrifice on our part.

Questions for Further Reflection

1. Consider the topic of spiritual investing—investing in people for the sake of the gospels and seeking to protect such spiritual investments. How would your life be different if you adopted this perspective?

15

Reflections on 3:6–10

The Source of Our Encouragement

A HELPFUL WINDOW INTO your heart is to consider what brings you comfort, strength and joy. What invigorates you? What gets you off your seat with excitement and joy? In 1 Thessalonians 3:6-10 Saint Paul highlights the overwhelming encouragement and pleasure he experiences when Timothy returns to share good news about the Thessalonians. Evidently what controls Paul's heart is the perseverance of the saints.

The good news Timothy conveys upon returning is that the Thessalonians are continuing in faith and love and long to see Paul and his colleagues (3:6). Despite persecution the Thessalonians have not given up the race of faith and have not forgotten those who had poured out their lives for their sake. As a result of their steadfastness in the Lord, Paul is deeply comforted in the affliction and suffering he himself is enduring and is renewed in his efforts to advance the gospel (3:7-8). Such is the profound impact our perseverance can have on others! It is a sobering thought that our faithfulness—or lack of—can have such an impact. This is something we need to be especially reminded of given the robust individualism rampant today.

Knowing that every blessing is from above, Paul immediately adds, "For what thanksgiving can we give back to God for you, for all the joy we have because of you before God? (3:9)" In doing so, he reminds us not to forget the Giver of every good gift. Finally, Paul reiterates his desire to see the Thessalonians face-to-face so that he may fill what is lacking in their faith (3:10). While rejoicing in their steadfastness, Paul knows that faith must receive continual nurture, which Paul will do in part through the rest of the letter especially in matters pertaining to the resurrection and Christ's second return. For this reason, acknowledging that all of life is under the sovereign rule of God, Paul communicates to the Thessalonians that he is praying earnestly for the opportunity to see them again.

Questions for Further Reflection

1. Where do you find joy and renewal? Does the faithfulness of other believers cause you to praise God? Does the faithlessness of professing Christians weigh down your spirit? Take some time to do some heart-exploration. Consider also the impact your own faithfulness—or lack of—has had on others. Are you intentional about considering the influence your perseverance has on other saints?

16

Reflections on 3:11–13

Life before God the Father and the Lord Jesus Christ

Saint Paul regularly prays both for "small" things (being able to visit the Thessalonians, 3:11), which seem too trivial for some to pray for, and "big" things (the strengthening of the saints, 3:12-13). In doing so he reminds us that all of life should be immersed in prayer because all of life involves communion with God.

In verses 12-13 Paul's prayer focuses on the inseparable tie between love and holiness. A life dedicated to honoring God certainly involves the pursuit of holiness. There is, however, the tendency to suppose that growing in holiness simply means sinning less. While holiness entails "not breaking the rules," it is much more. Growing in holiness must also include growing in love for all people, especially for the saints (3:12). God is love, as that has been manifested climactically in the sacrifice of His only beloved Son; hence, all who are in relationship with Him should pursue lives characterized by love. For this reason, if we discover in ourselves little compassion, we have cause to be concerned.

Verse 13 juxtaposes the presence of God ("before our God and Father") and the parousia ("the coming of our Lord Jesus with all his holy ones"). What this implies is that when the saints appear before God, they will also be standing before Jesus; which means that believers have a gracious Master and Savior currently interceding on their behalf. Throughout eternity the scars on Jesus' hands and feet serve as reminders that he was temporarily cast from the presence of God so that we might be forever welcome.

Questions for Further Reflection

1. Reflect on your prayer life. Do you pray regularly both for "small" and "big" things? In particular, do you pray for a deeper love for other believers? Moreover, do you pray in full conviction that you already have an exalted Savior who is currently interceding on your behalf?

17

Reflections on 4:1–2

Living to Please God

The phrase "living purposefully" is another way of saying living to please God, which should be the goal of every person who has turned from idols to serve the living and true God (1:9). The motivation, of course, is not to achieve salvation or to earn favor, but simply to please the One who has already saved us in Jesus and bestowed upon us favor unending. The mindset of a Christian is not dissimilar to that of a child who knows she is loved and cherished by her parents. This child is not obedient in order to curry their favor but to express her gratitude and joy for them.

Saint Paul suggests two practical applications for pursuing a life that is pleasing to God. First, such a life requires nurturing the habit of remembering. Twice in this brief passage Paul makes reference to this: "even as you received from us how you ought to walk and please God" (4:1b) and "You know what commands we gave to you through the Lord Jesus" (4:2). Many professing believers seem to leave their faith at the doorsteps of their church after Sunday service. On the given Sunday they will refrain from cursing, being unpleasant, and getting drunk on wine and pleasure. But all their piety is quickly forgotten the minute they step back into the "real" world. It should not surprise us, therefore, that the basic requisite for living a life pleasing to God is to remember the teaching, exhortations and reproofs we have received from our spiritual mentors and teachers.

An important aside is that God's will is revealed through the apostle to the saints. That is, it appears that God adopts the pattern of communicating to believers in general through specific individuals. Thus, Paul highlights the importance of remembering his teaching and instruction instead of pursuing individual revelation from God. Similarly, in their pursuit of God's will believers today would benefit greatly if they focused on the revelation that has already been given to us in the Holy Scriptures.

Second, a life pleasing to God requires the encouragement and inspiration of other believers. Believers today need the input of godly mentors and friends in their zeal to please the Lord. It is not enough—in fact, it is dangerous—to suppose God is pleased with me so long as I believe that that is the case. In God's wisdom we have been placed in community so that we might grow in our ability to please him through the exhortations and reproofs of other believers.

Questions for Further Reflection

1. How are you living intentionally to facilitate a lifestyle of remembering the truths and exhortations you have received from your spiritual leaders? In addition, are you purposeful in finding godly mentors and friends who speak truth into your life?

18

Reflections on 4:3–5

Living to Please God through Sexual Purity

"What is God's will for my life?" Perhaps you have asked this question; surely you have heard this question asked. This question is usually posed in relation to the big life questions of vocation and romance. There is little evidence in the Bible that suggests God provides explicit answers to such questions. Rather, it appears that God gives the basic "groove" for life from which we are to use our mind and the counsel of godly community to make such decisions. According to Saint Paul, God's "groove"—that is, his will for all believers—is their "sanctification" (4:3a), their being morally distinct from their surrounding world as a result of their union with Christ Jesus. Because in Christ Jesus they are now citizens of a new era marked by life and the Spirit, they are to set themselves apart accordingly.

Paul begins his discussion on sanctification by addressing the topic of sexual purity (4:3b). Much like our world today, Thessalonica suffered from no shortage of promiscuity. Intense sexual activity was rife not only in the seaport areas but also in many of the Greco-Roman cults. Paul's exhortation, therefore, to "withdraw from *porneai*" (a Greek word referring to any sexual activity outside of marriage) would have markedly set apart the Thessalonian believers from their associates. This exhortation is certainly no less relevant today for Christians who find themselves in a world where *porneai* is not only considered acceptable but also encouraged.

Instead of engaging in *porneai*, the Thessalonians are to find spouses and treat their marriages with holiness and honor (4:4). In other words, they are to pursue monogamous relationships. To do otherwise would suggest that they are still like the Gentiles, who do not know God and live to satisfy their lustful desires (4:5). In short, Paul is challenging his audience to adopt a view of sex and marriage that deviated radically from what they once considered normal. Again, this challenge is equally applicable today given the way people ridicule 40 year old virgins, hook up with strangers, and dismiss Christian views as prudish and outdated.

Bible scholars believe 1 Thessalonians was one of Paul's earliest letters; yet his view on the subject remained constant throughout his ministry. This suggests that from very early on the apostle came to a definitive stance on the matter and taught and lived accordingly. Similarly, those of us who have been purified through the blood of Christ and seek to please God must arrive at clear convictions on sex and marriage. God's will for our lives is to avoid *porneia* and to pursue monogamy. Living intentionally before God, then, undoubtedly entails pursuing purity according to the grace God gives us through His Son, who has already made us clean and acceptable before God.

Questions for Further Reflection

1. God's will is for believers to be morally set apart because they are already set apart in Jesus Christ. Take some time to explore your views on sex and marriage. Do they reflect cultural norms or gospel-convictions? Do they align with your new identity as someone who has already been purified through the blood of Christ?

19

Reflections on 4:6–8

Living to Please God through Sexual Purity (cont.)

In verses 6-8 Saint Paul continues his overall discussion on sexual purity. He urges the Thessalonians "not to transgress and cheat his brother in this matter" (4:6a). The command here is an extension of his exhortation on monogamy (4:4). The command implies that when we have sex outside of marriage, we are transgressing the sacred boundaries established by God. More to the point, with each person we have sex with outside of marriage, we are cheating that person's future spouse of his or her sacred union. In the sense, Paul views sex outside of marriage as a form of theft.

Paul knows his instructions represent not just a different perspective but a minority perspective. Even today many would laugh at and scorn what Paul says here. For this reason Paul reminds the Thessalonians that "God has not called us to impurity but to holiness" (4:7). Even when everyone else believes it is perfectly acceptable to have sex outside of marriage with as many people as possible, Christians are to be intentional about honoring the boundaries that God has established. This, again, is not in order to make themselves acceptable to God but because they already belong to the family of God through Jesus Christ. Despite whatever sexual impulse others possess, Christians find their cue from their Lord and Savior who has both made them holy and called them to holiness.

Of course it would have been easy for the Thessalonians to dismiss Paul's exhortation in this matter as merely the opinion of one individual. Perhaps their peers asked why they were depriving themselves of so much sexual gratification on account of one person's words. Paul's response is, "Whoever rejects this command does not reject man but God, who gives us his Spirit who is holy" (4:8). Echoing 2:13, Paul reminds the Thessalonians that he is not merely imposing his personal beliefs and preferences on them, but speaking on behalf of God, whose desire is for them to be holy even as the Spirit of Christ is in them is holy. We cannot, then, claim to want to do the will of God and yet disregard the explicit guidelines God has given through His appointed apostle.

The solemn tone of Paul's instruction indicates that sex and marriage are no laughing matters. His seriousness is not intended to take away from the pleasure that sexual union brings in marriage. But the gravity of his tone suggests that the full extent of sexual pleasure in marriage is realized only when it is taken seriously. Thus, this text invites us to be purposeful in the way we think about and engage in sex. May God grant us much grace to please Him in this area where temptation knows no bounds!

Questions for Further Reflection

1. Are you purposeful about adopting a radically different ethic with respect to sex and marriage? Reflect on how you rob others by becoming physically intimate with their current or future spouse. Do you take the apostle's instructions as God's own commands or dismiss them as merely the opinions of an individual? Are you serious in your pursuit of sexual pleasure?

20

Reflections on 4:9–10

Living to Please God through Brotherly Love

Everyone agrees there is nothing more powerful than family ties. Parents make incredible sacrifices for their children; siblings cover one another's sins; husbands and wives persevere in love. Such is the power of family! The gospel, however, challenges us to reconsider our views on whom we consider family. We are not asked to abandon our biological family but to extend kinship to those whom we usually consider just friends or strangers. The expression "brotherly love" (4:9a) translates the Greek word *philadelphia*, a term found in ancient Greek literature to describe familial love. Saint Paul's use of the word is intentional for he is seeking to encourage the Thessalonians to view and love one another as family because of their common adoption through Jesus Christ.

Verse 10 indicates that they are already doing this by treating traveling Christians from Macedonia as "brothers." One can only imagine how difficult this must have been for the Thessalonians given they consisted of people from very different backgrounds. Much like believers today the Thessalonians had to overcome old ways of thinking which taught them to distinguish themselves on the basis of familial lines and economic status. Herein we find another example of how the gospel should effect radical change in our lives.

Paul reminds the Thessalonians that they "are God-taught to love one another" (4:9b). Here, he is not saying that they have been taught *to* love another—that they *should*—but *how* to do so. As God has loved them as their Heavenly Father and as Christ Jesus has loved them as the Faithful Brother, so too they are to love one another in a familial way. This sort of love has already been expressed concretely through Paul, Silvanus, and Timothy. The first half of chapter two rehearsed how Paul and his colleagues were like nursing mothers (2:7) and responsible fathers (2:11) throughout their ministry to the Thessalonians. In addition, the apostle's repeated use of "brothers" in the letter is not just rhetoric but an expression of his familial attitude towards the Thessalonians as a result of their common union in Christ Jesus.

The expression "to do this more" (4:10b) reiterates the command in 4:1 to guard against complacency. The expression captures a profound challenge. On the one hand, believers are to go beyond the cultural norm of viewing only biological kin as family members. On the other hand, they should not suppose they have "arrived" at accomplishing this great feat. Rather, they are to increase their love for one another, having experienced the overwhelming love of God in Christ Jesus. Such is the high calling for those who desire to pursue a life that is pleasing to God.

Questions for Further Reflection

1. Whom do you consider family? How are you challenged to think of family differently in light of the gospel? Are there Christians you would not consider family because of the color of their skin or because of their different socio-economic background? Consider ways you can increase your love for your new family in Christ Jesus.

21

Reflections on 4:11–12

Living to Please God through Respectable Conduct

Aware of their persecution, Saint Paul provides sound instruction in 4:11-12 on how believers are to relate to unbelievers under such difficult circumstances. In general Paul never promoted the notion of separating altogether from society. Rather, the people of God have always been called to be *in* the world though not *of* the world. Nevertheless, there are times when believers simply cannot directly engage the world. Under such circumstances the apostle provides the following words of encouragement.

First, the Thessalonians are instructed to "endeavor to live quietly and to mind their own affairs" (4:11a). Given the persecution they had already suffered, Paul's desire for them is to avoid further conflict by maintaining a low profile. The instruction "to mind their own affairs" (4:11a) is likely a reference to avoid patron-client systems that bound an individual to a patron who could make all sorts of unholy demands. In other words, Paul's counsel is to be wise—to discern the season—in order to minimize further eruptive situations. The apostle is fully aware that suffering is inevitable for followers of Jesus Christ. Nevertheless, he does not believe that Christians should pursue suffering itself. Rather, when possible, Christians should wisely consider which course of actions will facilitate general peace.

The other piece of instruction—to work hard with your own hands so that you are not dependent on another (4:11b-12)—echoes Paul's own example of laboring in order not to be a burden to others (2:9). By doing so, Paul was able to strengthen the suffering church—both by refusing income and by positioning himself to help those who were unable to work.

Seeking a life that is pleasing to God, then, involves being discerning and deciding what one should do—and not do—for the sake of the gospel. In other words, living intentionally means living wisely. Living intentionally perceives that sometimes the best way to honor God is to remain silent and allow our actions to communicate our convictions. Sometimes it means realizing that the best thing we can do for our church is enter a season of giving versus receiving.

Questions for Further Reflection

1. Living to please God—living intentionally—means living wisely. Consider Paul's instructions in today's passage as examples of what it means to "discern the season." What does living intentionally/living wisely look like for you here and now?

22

Reflections on 4:13–18

The Grand Reunion

We grow up hearing stories with happy endings, but eventually we grow out of these stories and adopt a more cynical outlook on life. Not unlike the Teacher from Ecclesiastes we begin to feel like everything is meaningless. In today's passage, however, Saint Paul seeks to encourage believers by reminding them of their happy ending. That Christian hope is intended to go beyond knowledge and shape our present experiences is suggested by the apostle's use of "believe" versus "know" in the beginning of verse 14.

The Thessalonians were concerned for those that had already died, possibly as a result of persecution. The passage reveals that they were not so much concerned about the ultimate fate of those who had "fallen asleep" but that such believers would not witness Christ's triumphant return. In response to these concerns, Paul comforts the Thessalonians by reminding them that God will raise to life those who have "fallen asleep" with the same power manifested in Jesus' resurrection (4:14). Paul then outlines the "resurrection-sequence": First, Christ will descend; second, the faithful who have already died will be raised to life; third, believers who are still alive will be caught up with the resurrected believers to meet the Lord in the air (4:15-17). In this sense Christ's return will be a grand reunion for all—from every place and every period—who have trusted in Christ Jesus for eternal life and have confessed Him as Lord.

Paul concludes this passage by commanding the Thessalonians to encourage one another with these truths (4:18)—all the more because his words are not the words of a human being but of the Lord Jesus Christ (4:15a). Specifically, they are to encourage one another to "grieve well"—to grieve differently from those who do not have such a hope. This life, as every believer knows, will not be sheltered from pain and suffering just because we have trusted in Jesus for salvation. In fact, as Paul has already indicated in the letter, suffering is inevitable for Christians. Knowing this—but also believing in the glory that is ours through Christ—we are called to grieve "intentionally"—to weep and cry while anticipating this grand reunion.

Questions for Further Reflection

1. Reflect on the picture presented in 4:16-17. How does this picture of resurrection-glory encourage you in your current suffering? How does it inspire you to grieve "intentionally"? What would this look like in your life? What impact do you think this would have on others?

23

Reflections on 5:1–11

Hopeful People

The opening verses of chapter five address some basic points concerning Christians and the future. On the one hand, Saint Paul reminds all believers that no one knows "the Day of the Lord," for it will come unexpectedly "like a thief in the night" and suddenly as "labor pains come upon a pregnant woman" (5:1-3). For this reason, we should not pay attention to those who claim to know when the world will end. In fact, we ought to be very wary of such persons, given they often claim to be prophets. The Bible makes absolutely clear that no one knows when the Day of the Lord will come.

On the other hand, Paul reminds believers that even though they do not know the timing of Jesus' return, they know its reality; hence, they should not at all be surprised when it happens as if they were in darkness (5:4-5). Much in the way we do not know the exact hour a storm will begin, we know nevertheless that it will come and so should not be surprised when it does. We must not become overly comfortable, supposing "peace and security" will go unchecked. Basking in comfort and thereby forgetting that God's wrath is coming is just as dangerous as believing that the Day is right around the corner.

We are told further to "keep awake and be sober," as is fitting for those who are children of light (5:6). Specifically, Paul exhorts believers to put on the helmet, which is "the hope of salvation" (5:8).

Christian hope is that we will escape the coming wrath through Jesus Christ, "who died for us so that whether we are awake or asleep we might live with him" (5:9-10). In short, our future is set regardless of what happens in the present because of the perfect and finished work of Jesus Christ. Hallelujah! To put on the helmet, then, is to protect against allowing present difficulties to evaporate our hope of salvation. As Jesus said on the cross, "It is finished." Our salvation has been secured through His blood; thus, while we do not know when the Day of the Lord will come, we can be confident that it will be day of gladness and joy. With such precious truths concerning the future, we are to build one another up to live intentionally as those whose eternal destiny has already been secured through Christ's perfect life, death, and resurrection.

Questions for Further Reflection

1. Which extreme do you tend to err towards? Are you attracted to those who try to figure out when the world will end? Or are you prone to forget that the Day of the Lord is coming? As someone who has trusted in Christ's atoning work for salvation, does your life exude joy and excitement as you anticipate His return?

24

Reflections on 5:12–13

Respecting Those in Authority

One has probably observed two extremes when it comes to authority. There are those who revere those in authority. Then there are those who—at best—treat them as equals if not with contempt. Whether our attitude and actions are based on our cultural upbringing or personal experiences, the Bible challenges us be thoughtful and intentional about the way we understand and relate to authority in the church.

Twice in the passage Saint Paul exhorts the Thessalonians to honor those in authority. He specifies that they should do so because of the "work" such leaders do (5:12-13), not because of any socio-economic status they might have (although this was likely the case for the Thessalonian leaders). Although positions of authority often appear attractive and desirable, leading well is an extraordinarily onerous task, especially because it includes the work of admonishing. Almost no one likes receiving criticism or even feedback; yet, the duty of church leaders often requires pointing out sin and calling believers to repentance. In addition, authentic church leaders constantly feel the weight of their work; after all eternal souls are at stake.

Therefore, those of us under authority ought to make every effort to honor our spiritual shepherds. They are, after all, people whom Christ has placed to preserve truth and promote order in the household of God. Ultimately, our submission to those in authority—assuming they themselves are submitting to the authority of Christ—is an expression of our submission to Christ's lordship over our own lives.

At the end of verse 13 the apostle adds a word on striving to maintain peace. Paul likely has in mind potential divisions as they relate to leadership. We are reminded of the situation in Corinthians where there was quarreling among the saints with some saying, "I follow Paul," and others, "I follow Apollos," and so forth. There may also have been some resentment and rivalry as leaders emerged in the young congregations of Thessalonica. Whether Paul is concerned about avoiding factions or rivalries—or both—his point is that believers should always seek peace amongst themselves, an exhortation especially relevant to the Thessalonians who could not afford internal strife given the external persecution they were already suffering.

Beginning with chapter four, Paul has described a life that is pleasing to God. Today's passage is a reminder that pleasing God includes something as seemingly mundane and ordinary as respecting our church leaders and seeking to maintain peace. Despite whatever negative personal experiences we have had or unhealthy reverence we have observed, the biblical teaching is clear that living purposefully before God entails relating properly to those in spiritual authority.

Questions for Further Reflection

1. What is your tendency when it comes to relating to those in authority, especially church leaders? How does today's passage affirm or challenge your disposition? What are some ways you are currently dishonoring your church leaders? What are some ways you are currently honoring your church leaders? Consider ways you can help keep peace at your local church, especially as it relates to the leadership.

25

Reflections on 5:14–15

Actively Loving One Another

When it comes to loving people—especially fellow believers—we must never suppose that we have arrived, as if there is no room for growth and improvement. In fact, as we grow in our understanding and experience of God's love in Christ Jesus, we see how we ought to love others better. Saint Paul indicates some of these ways in today's passage. They include warning others of inappropriate behavior; encouraging those who have low self-esteem; remembering the physically weak; being patient; and seeking grace over retribution (5:14-15). These are all ways Christ loved people during his earthly ministry and now challenges his discipleship to do likewise. It is worthwhile to reflect on these specific exhortations and consider ways to apply them concretely and regularly. In what follows, however, I want to comment on some implications from these exhortations.

First, Paul assumes that each member of the church will play an active role in the sanctification of the overall community. He does not suppose that the growth of the church is just the work of those in spiritual authority. The members themselves are expected to point out sin and call one another to repentance; to encourage the fainthearted; to help the physically weak; and to abound in grace. To be sure, those in authority play a unique role in leading church members; but this does not mean the latter group should adopt a passive stance. We are, after all, one body in Christ Jesus; thus each member is to do its part in building up the entire body.

Second, Paul assumes that the members actually know one another. They know if people are living in sin; they know those who struggle with insecurity; they know one another's physical ailments; they know when others are tempted to act vindictively. Many professing Christians today are tempted to join large churches where they can remain anonymous: they neither want to be known nor want to know others. Against this tendency Paul expects them to be investing time and energy into one another's lives so that, in turn, they are able to care for one another well. This call to take steps to know one another is simply an imitation of how Christ became a man to know the suffering of mankind in order to redeem it from the power of sin.

Finally—and most importantly—believers are to relate to one another the way God has related to them in Jesus Christ. Because God loves us, he disciplines us in our sins so that we might fear Him and walk according to His ways. When our souls are downcast, He lifts us up by the power of His Spirit and the promises of the gospel. He heals those who are broken, both physically and emotionally. And He is always long-suffering, giving kindness to those who deserve nothing but wrath. In this sense, the call to honor one another is an invitation to do to one another what God has first done for us in Christ Jesus.

Questions for Further Reflection

1. Consider ways you can practice the exhortations listed by Saint Paul. How might viewing these specific exhortations as ways God has loved us in Christ Jesus inspire and empower us to love one another with grace and perseverance?

26

Reflections on 5:16–18

The Praying Life

In the Book of Genesis we are given a beautiful picture of what fellowship with God originally looked like. Genesis 3:8a reads, "And they heard the sound of the Lord God walking in the garden in the cool of the day." What this implies is that Adam and Eve were accustomed to walking and talking with the Lord. Other Old Testament references confirm this (see Genesis 5:21-24). Similarly, Saint Paul reminds the Thessalonians that God's will for them is to renew this sort of intimate relationship with God by focusing on three aspects of prayer—rejoicing, asking, and giving thanks.

Verse 16 begins with the adverb "always," recalling the preceding exhortation "to always seek to do the good to one another" (5:15). The earlier exhortation is a subtle reminder of how God did not punish us according to our sins but extended mercy and goodness to us through the death and resurrection of Christ. The first part of prayer, then, is a call to always rejoice because of the salvation that God has given to us through Jesus Christ. The context of persecution makes clear that the Thessalonians are facing less than ideal circumstances that might have led to despair. Paul reminds them, however, that their salvation is powerful enough to enable them to rejoice always.

In addition to always rejoicing, Paul exhorts believers to constantly pray—to bring their requests and supplications to God, and in all things to give thanks (5:17-18). There is nothing that we should feel is above or beneath God to hear. Sometimes we think that a particular concern is too silly for God to even consider; or, ironically, we suppose that a given situation is beyond God's power to handle. But the gospel reminds us that God is the almighty Father who has adopted us through the atoning work of Christ Jesus. Therefore, He not only cares to hear the little things but has sufficient power to raise the dead and to answer our prayers. Finally, Paul reminds us not only to ask God for things but also to thank him in all circumstances, as Paul modeled in 1:2 and 2:13. The phrase "in all circumstances" echoes 5:16, reminding us all that there is, indeed, always a reason to be thankful as those who are no longer under the wrath of God, a truth easily forgotten in times of suffering and persecution.

While these verses focus on the importance of prayer, they reflect God's gracious invitation for us to walk and talk with him. The purpose of salvation is not simply or even primarily to "get out of hell," but to enjoy the One who has made it possible for us to come again before His presence through Jesus Christ. Living an intentional life, then, is not just about living *for* Him but *with* Him each step of the way. This is God's will for us in Christ Jesus.

Questions for Further Reflection

1. Reflect on the three aspects of prayer Paul lists in these verses. How can growing in any one of these deepen your personal walk with God? Meditate on how living intentionally includes both living for God and living with Him.

27

Reflections on 5:19–22

Listening to the Spirit

ALL HEALTHY CONVERSATIONS ASSUME both parties are talking and listening. 1 Thessalonians 5:16-18 highlighted the importance of speaking to God about everything: in his unfathomable grace God invites us to speak to Him about all aspects of our lives. Verses 19-22 now focus on listening to what God says to believers through believers; and it does so in a balanced way, addressing those who are inclined to reject prophetic utterances as well as those who are overly zealous to receive them.

In 5:19-20 Saint Paul urges the Thessalonians not to be unduly skeptical about prophecies. It appears that they were quenching the Spirit's words by treating them with contempt. There is little detail that helps explain this particular reaction to prophecies that runs opposite to the Corinthians' fascination with the spiritual gifts. Whatever the reason was for their disdain, Paul makes clear they should not hinder the practice of prophetic speaking.

Paul, however, does not promote a thoughtless acceptance of all prophecies. Rather, he exhorts the Thessalonians to test them much in the way precious metals were tested and approved (5:21a). Prophecies, after all, can be true and edifying or false and destructive depending on the source. This is an apt warning, given there is the tendency not only to be skeptical but also uncritical. True prophecies conform to revelation that has been given explicitly and clearly through Christ and His apostles and always result in the edification of the saints, as Paul's own ministry demonstrated.

Finally, believers are to act upon the prophecies either by "holding fast to what is good" (5:21b) or "abstaining from every kind of evil" (5:22). On the one hand, in their pursuit of living a life that is pleasing to God it is necessary to hold fast to what has proven true and healthy for the saints. On the other hand, as believers are to abstain from every kind of sexual impurity (4:3), so too they are to avoid all species of prophecies that contradict the gospel of God concerning Christ Jesus. In summary, a life that is pleasing to God requires being intentional about what one pays attention to and what one altogether shuns.

Questions for Further Reflection

1. What is your "prophetic bias"? Are you inclined to despise them like the Thessalonians or to obsess over them like the Corinthians? How does today's passage move you towards a more biblical balance? What concrete steps can you take to be either more open or more cautious?

28

Reflections on 5:23–24

Our True Hope

In a most fitting way Saint Paul precedes his closing requests (5:25-27) with a prayer of blessing, focusing the Thessalonians on the God who has already accomplished peace through Jesus Christ. Beginning with 4:1, the apostle highlighted the believer's role in sanctification, reminding us that we cannot be passive about our own transformation and growth. Nevertheless, lest there is even an inkling of thought that our sanctification and salvation ultimately depend on us the apostle concludes the letter by focusing on God's initiative and faithfulness to every good work He begins.

As Paul stated plainly, the will of God is our sanctification (4:3a); and here Paul makes clear that it is God himself who will accomplish this ("May the God of peace *himself* sanctify you *completely*," 5:23a). This prayer echoes the earlier benediction where the apostle prayed that God would increase the Thessalonians' love for one another (3:11-13). It should not surprise us, then, that sanctification is always tied to deeper affections for the saints, resulting in peace between all believers. There is no way around it: sanctification, love, and peace are all interconnected, such that the absence of one suggests the absence of the others.

Keeping in mind the Thessalonians' suffering and persecution, Paul also prays that their entire being—their spirit, soul, and body—would be kept blameless until the coming of the Lord Jesus Christ; that is, that the Thessalonians would persevere in their faith in the face of danger and rejection. The use of the passive "be kept" here is intentional, reiterating that even their faithfulness is ultimately the result of God's own faithfulness to them, expressed in terms of power through His Spirit. Indeed, as the great hymn declares, "Twas grace that brought us safe thus far and grace will lead us home."

Verse 24 concludes the benediction with the uplifting words: "Faithful is the One who calls you, and He will surely do it." Indeed, it is God who not only calls believers to be holy but God who is faithful to complete every good work He starts (Philippians 1:6). Amidst our failures and doubts we have the sure hope that the One who calls is faithful even as such faithfulness was demonstrated in Christ's own resurrection from the dead. Thus Paul—redundantly but pastorally—emphasizes that God will accomplish their salvation. This is the sure foundation upon which an intentional life is built. Because believers have the sure hope of vindication, perfection, and glorification—because they know their efforts will never be in vain—they can pursue an intentional life characterized by joy, hope, and love.

Question for Further Reflection

1. Given sanctification, love, and peace are all interconnected, what might the absence of one suggest concerning the others? Do you find that you're growing in all three areas? Meditate on the truth captured wonderfully in the lyrics, "Twas grace that brought us safe thus far and grace will lead us home." How does this truth encourage and empower your soul to faithfulness?

29

Reflections on 5:25–28

Living Intentionally Now

Saint Paul concludes the letter with several exhortations and a blessing. At a first glance, they appear somewhat random. A closer look, however, shows that they relate very much to what Paul has written in the letter. Thus, the apostle is effectively giving the Thessalonians the opportunity to put into practice the things he has just commanded, that is, to live intentionally now.

The first exhortation is to pray for Paul, Timothy, and Silvanus (5:25), a clear application of the praying life as outlined in 5:16-18. We should be humbled by Paul's request for prayer. In this life there is no person who is never in need of prayer, even—or perhaps especially—those who appear to be spiritual giants. The second exhortation is to greet all the brothers with a holy kiss (5:26). Such greetings should be extended to all who now belong to the family of God (4:9-12). In addition, the kiss should be holy (4:3-8), reflecting our new status in Christ Jesus as holy-ones who can now stand before the presence of a holy God. The final exhortation is for the letter to be read to all the brothers (5:27). This likely suggests the presence of multiple house churches in Thessalonica, but it may also be a subtle reminder that Paul's words should be read to all versus a limited and perhaps elite group. Through such unconventional social bonds the Thessalonians can place the gospel of God on display for all the world to see.

All this, however, is impossible apart from God's empowering grace. We not only need to know God's will for our lives, but we also require the power to do so. There are many today who believe that knowledge alone can redeem the world. The Bible, however, underscores our need for grace to be and do what we would not be and do left to ourselves. We need the Savior, therefore, just the same today as we did yesterday and as we will forever more. And so may we continue to look to our Lord Jesus Christ for wisdom and power as we pursue an intentional life before Him and for Him!

Questions for Further Reflection

1. What opportunities for obeying God are immediately available to you? What is hindering you from practicing the will of God? Who are the people you should be praying for? Who are the people you should be greeting? Who are the people you should be sharing the gospel with? Are you pursuing God for more grace in order to do His will?